First Facts™

Everyday Character Education

Courage

by Kristin Thoennes Keller

Consultant:
Madonna Murphy, PhD, Professor of Education
University of St. Francis, Joliet, Illinois
Author, *Character Education in America's Blue Ribbon Schools*

Capstone
press
Mankato, Minnesota

First Facts is published by Capstone Press,
151 Good Counsel Drive, P.O. Box 669, Mankato, Minnesota 56002.
www.capstonepress.com

Library of Congress Cataloging-in-Publication Data
Thoennes Keller, Kristin.
Courage / by Kristin Thoennes Keller.
    p. cm.—(First facts. Everyday character education)
    ISBN 0-7368-3679-9 (hardcover)
    ISBN 0-7368-5147-X (paperback)
    1. Courage—Juvenile literature. I. Title. II. Series: First facts. Everyday character education.
BJ1533.C8T48 2005
179'.6—dc22   2004018351

Summary: Introduces courage through examples of everyday situations where this character trait
    can be used.

Editorial Credits
Amanda Doering, editor; Molly Nei, set designer; Kia Adams, book designer; Wanda Winch,
    photo researcher

Photo Credits
Gem Photo Studio/Dan Delaney, cover, 1, 5, 6–7, 8, 9, 10–11, 12, 13, 19
Corbis/Bettmann, 16-17
Noah Hamilton Photography, 15
Photo Researchers Inc./Dick Luria, 13 (broken glass)
Schlesinger Library, Radcliffe Institute, Harvard University, 20

Table of Contents

Courage

Taylor and her friend sign up for camp together. The day before camp starts, Taylor's friend breaks her arm. Taylor is afraid to go to camp alone. She doesn't think she'll have fun without her friend. Taylor shows courage. She goes to camp anyway. She has fun and makes new friends.

Fact!
Courage is the strength to try something new, even if it is difficult.

At Your School

Students need courage at school. Other students may ask you to do something wrong. Be courageous and do the right thing. If someone asks to **cheat** off your paper, tell him no.

Sticking up for someone takes courage. If students are teasing kids at school, tell them to stop.

With Your Friends

Friends might want you to do something dangerous or wrong. It takes courage to say no. Saying no can keep you from getting hurt or into trouble.

Courageous friends aren't afraid to say they're sorry. If you hurt a friend, **apologize**. **Admitting** you are wrong takes courage.

At Home

Show courage at home.
Use courage to talk to
your parents about your
brother or sister. If your
sister is doing something
dangerous, tell a parent.
Your sister may get into
trouble with your parents,
but she will be safe.

In Your Community

Courageous people are good neighbors. Welcome new kids on your street. Talking to new people takes courage.

Courageous people admit their mistakes. If you break a neighbor's window, tell him. You may be afraid, but do what is right.

Bethany Hamilton

When she was 13 years old, Bethany Hamilton was attacked by a shark while surfing. Bethany lost her arm in the attack. Ten weeks after the attack, Bethany was surfing again. Bethany showed courage by getting back on her surfboard. She didn't let her **injury** stop her from surfing.

Fact!

Being courageous does not mean taking dangerous risks. Courageous people know their limits.

Amelia Earhart

Amelia Earhart was a U.S. pilot. She lived in the early 1900s. Earhart showed courage by flying her plane alone, or **solo**. In 1932, she became the first woman to fly across the Atlantic Ocean alone. Earhart showed courage by doing something no woman had done before.

Fact!

In 1937, Earhart's plane disappeared over the ocean. She and her plane have never been found.

What Would You Do?

Taylor is a good speller. She knows she would do well in the school spelling bee. But Taylor is afraid. She doesn't like speaking in front of people. She wants to skip the spelling bee. What is the courageous thing for Taylor to do?

Fact!
Many people fear speaking in front of people more than they fear dying.